T0380159

BE

TIFUL

AN INSPIRATIONAL AND EMPOWERING COLLECTION OF POEMS AND AFFIRMATIONS

Written by

EBUN OLADEJO

© 2022 Ebun Oladejo. All rights reserved.

No part of this book may be reproduced, stored in a retrieval system,
or transmitted by any means without the written permission of the author.

AuthorHouse™
1663 Liberty Drive
Bloomington, IN 47403
www.authorhouse.com
Phone: 833-262-8899

Because of the dynamic nature of the Internet, any web addresses or links contained in this book may have changed
since publication and may no longer be valid. The views expressed in this work are solely those of the author and do not
necessarily reflect the views of the publisher, and the publisher hereby disclaims any responsibility for them.

Front Cover Designed by Daniel Oladejo

All Scripture quotations are taken from New Living Translation (NLT) Holy Bible, New Living Translation, copyright © 1996, 2004, 2015
by Tyndale House Foundation. Used by permission of Tyndale House Publishers, Inc., Carol Stream, Illinois 60188. All rights reserved.

This book is printed on acid-free paper.

ISBN: 978-1-6655-7353-5 (sc)
ISBN: 978-1-6655-7352-8 (e)

Print information available on the last page.

Published by AuthorHouse 10/03/2023

Contact us:
Website: https://www.ebunoladejo.com/
Email: ceddbyebun@gmail.com

authorHOUSE®

To the Almighty God who created, equipped, designed, and
destined me with the great power of speech.
To my family, friends, fathers and mothers of faith, mentors, coaches, and teachers whose
graces I enjoy, and, on whose shoulders, I ride to become a better version of myself.
To the scars of those who believed in my purpose and were open,
vulnerable, and secure to lead me with their pains.
To coach Queen Lova Bassong who saw a book in my manuscript and
Aunty Pamela Egbe-Messy who read and arranged the content…
The dream has become a reality. This is your *crown*.
Thank you!

CONTENTS

PREFACE

I have had moments of pain, fear, failure, low self-esteem, self-doubt, crisis, and distress in my life. The thought of *where do I go from here?* gave me sleepless nights and anxieties, but the Almighty God was ever there for me. He picked me up from the lowest depth and gave me strength to reach into the highest heights through the power of spoken words.

As a result of my life experiences, I relate with people through the lens of love, compassion, and empathy. I see and believe that each person is **C**reated, **E**quipped, **D**esigned, and **D**estined to *become* what they were born to be if watered with the right words for reset, refreshment, and renewal of their minds.

Words mean more than what is written down on paper. It will take a voice to give life to words. So, this life-changing book comprising of encouragements, poems, and affirmations will help you use your voice to reinforce your words.

As you read and speak the words in this book over the course of sixty days, make it the life-giving transfusion you need for daily blessing, healing, and empowerment. Take ownership of the words, and let them kick start your morning, boost your afternoon, and calm your evening.

Be YOUtiful. Thrive in your purpose!

DAY 1

You are created in God's image, equipped with God's reflection, designed into God's purpose, and destined for God's glory.

A Firm Introduction

I am blessed, I am highly favored.

I am rich, I am wealthy.

I am the head and not the tail.

I am wonderful, I am remarkable, I am loved.

I am a brilliant wife; I am a wonderful mother.

I am peace, I am joy, I am hope.

I am not confused—I have clarity.

I am not tired, as I have a purpose.

I am the toughest warrior on the front line.

I will not give in nor give up; I will win all my battles.

I will triumph in life, and I will reach my destination.

I am strong, I am confident, I am breaking through.

I am articulate, I am wise; I am healed, I am alive.

I am the best version of myself today.

I am a champion. I will not die: I will live,

For I am resilient, bold, and courageous.

Day 2

You are created with your own unique light. You are equipped with your own radiance. You are designed with your own sparkle. You are destined to shine your own spirit!

A Spirit Credential

I am a child of God.

I know my rights.

I do exploits.

I am a strong nation.

I am a thousand times larger.

I am like the palm tree;

I am like the cedar of Lebanon.

I am a fruitful and useful field.

I have the Spirit of the Lord in me.

I have the Spirit of Wisdom and Understanding.

I am filled with the Spirit of Counsel and Might.

I operate with the Spirit of Knowledge.

I live with the Spirit of the Fear of the Lord.

I am endowed with grace and glory.

I have the visionary eye of an eagle.

I have the gentleness of a dove.

I have the meekness of a lamb.
I have the strength of a unicorn.
I have the patience of an ass.
I have the boldness of a lion.
I have the wisdom of the Ancient.
My path is like a shining light:
I shine brighter and brighter,
Until I reach my goal.

DAY 3

I'm an epitome of beauty, an excellence of royalty, an example of Christianity.

A Victor's Confession

My best days are right in front of me:
Mistakes are turned to miracles;
Losses, to gains.

Sickness is turned to health;
Death, to life.
My sorrow is turned to joy.

Darkness has brought forth light.
Shame has become fame,
My gladness fully restored.

I am no more a liability.
I have been promoted to a personality,
Celebrated for my tenacity,
And honored into the circle of royalty.

Now I know those moments of pain,
Were to prepare me for these seasons of rain,
Where I now live to long enjoy
Everything I once endured.

DAY 4

As long as the sun shines, as long as the river flows, as long as the grass grows, my destiny of PURPOSE *is guaranteed.*

I Am Me

I may not have the same qualifications as you, but I am Me.

I may not have had your kind of life experiences, yet I am Me.

I may not even belong to your esteemed social status; still, I am Me.

I may not be financially buoyant and materially affluent like you, I am Me!

I am a child of God.

I am the real deal.

I am Indescribable.

I am Indestructible.

I am Indomitable.

I am Inestimable.

I am Irreplaceable.

I am Irresistible.

I am Incredibly authentic.

I am my own kind of beautiful,

Created, equipped, designed, destined.

I am the unique Me,

I am the elegant Me—

I really love Me!

Day 5

When you don't get a miracle, God can still use you as a miracle for someone else.

Be You: Life's Credo

As you take your journey through this world,
you will have in your life, or meet along the way,
people who might want to eat you up.
Be You!

They do everything within their power
to make you small, and if they fail,
they try to define you by their own expectations.
Be You!

Sometimes they mischaracterize you,
misunderstand you and misjudge you.
Ignore every bit of it.
Be You!

Child of God, be your own authentic self.
Know yourself, and if you are lost,
get back to yourself.
Be You!

Raise your head up, square your shoulders, and walk.
I mean walk elegantly, walk majestically, walk courageously.
Do not look back; focus on the goal.
Be You!

Keep walking forward, failing forward,
changing forward, thrusting forward,
and soaring higher.
Be You!

You are created, equipped, designed, and destined
for such a time as this.
Be You!

Day 6

God created, equipped, designed, and destined you with everything you need to reach unimaginable heights. Let your greatness find expression.

My Decision through God

Oh, I woke up early this morning,

My heart beating right on time,

And said, "Lord, I really thank You

For giving me life today."

Then I went over to my mirror

To behold how wonderfully I'm made.

I dressed up, stepped out, and showed up,

Declaring these words as I went:

"I will take steps that will make me relevant in all aspects of life.

I will challenge myself so that my knowledge will not be obsolete.

I will learn, unlearn, and relearn.

I will walk the talk and stay on the cutting edge."

Day 7

You are destined for global recognition. Keep moving.

Equipped

You are equipped with influence;

You are endowed with affluence.

Don't stay where you are tolerated;

Move to the place where you are celebrated.

Be surrounded by those who recognize your emergence;

Go to those who receive your existence.

Pour yourself into those who are delighted in your power,

And strengthen those who believe in your purpose.

I see you at the top!

DAY 8

Do not allow those who were not there when God spoke to you make you feel horrible for obeying a divine order! Remember, Abraham obeyed what sounded foolish. So long as it is God, obey without explanation to anyone.

Praise Is What I Do; Worship Is Who I Am

I am a created being, made in the image of God.
I am a wonder on earth, sent as a masterpiece.
I am a voice to the world, with many sounds of adoration.
Praise is what I do; worship is who I am.

I am an equipped vessel, empowered to speak the Word.
I am endowed with so much grace to sing psalms and hymns.
I am filled with the Holy Spirit with the anointing to function.
Praise is what I do; worship is who I am.

I am designed so fearfully, made colorful and wonderful.
I am here to lead others to Christ, help them to find the Lord.
I am decorated with so much beauty to introduce the splendor of the King.
Praise is what I do; worship is who I am.

I am destined to a life of sacrifice, spreading on the throne day and night.

I am surrendered before His glory, declaring His awesome majesty.

I am the one on the winning side, dancing more than David danced.

Praise is what I do; worship is who I am.

Praise is what I do; worship is who I am.

Praise is what I do; worship is who I am.

Praise is what I do; worship is who I am.

DAY 9

Today is for you. Wake up. Dress up. Step out. Step up. Stride. Roar. Soar.

Go Ahead—Don't Look Back!

Wow! Look at you,

Emperor, conqueror, dogged, daring—

You're destined to take the world

And color it with your creative mix.

Go for it. Go for it!

Let the giant in you ARISE!

Let the champion in you WALK!

Let the lion in you ROAR!

Let the greatness in you EMERGE!

Go ahead, EVOLVE—

Don't look back.

Don't be tempted to—?

Keep your focus as you go.

I see you at the top!

Day 10

The attitude with which you start a new day determines the altitude of the day.
Always plan to win, prepare to win, expect to win, and celebrate your win.

I Want to Be the Rainbow

I want to be a RAINBOW
In somebody's CLOUD.
I want to be the ANSWER
To somebody's QUESTION.
Lord I ask to be the JOY
In somebody's SORROW,
And I pray to be a BLESSING
In somebody's LIFE today.

Day 11

The Blood of Jesus turns brokenness to beauty, and His grace causes a blooming throughout the seasons.

See, I Am Elegant!

Although I have not always had an easy life,
My journey to greatness hasn't been all rosy,
My walk with God hasn't been all smooth,
Nor has any victory come without a fight,

Trials and challenges have come my way,
And difficulties have shaken my very world,
Yet in Christ the solid rock I stand,
Because I know who I am and whose I am.

God says I am chosen, royal, holy, peculiar.
He says I am pleasingly graceful, stylish in appearance and manner.
God says I am competent, confident, compassionate.
He says I glow and radiate with respectable reputation.

So it doesn't matter what *others* think or say,
Just take a good look at me yet again:
See, I *am* elegant.

Day 12

You will fall, you will fail, your faith will be tested. Just stand firm! Face the world unashamed, continue to sing the song of freedom. God's mercy will favor you.

A Rising Phoenix

I am a rising phoenix.
I am a symbol of renewal and rebirth,
I am an epitome of beauty and grace.

I emerge from ashes,
I arise from destruction,
I recover from losses.

I am a rising phoenix.
I bring hope to every being,
I give strength to any doing,
I keep up the human spirit.
I am a do-without in the world.

Day 13

When you step out there, raise your head high. Smile! Stride! Soar!
Reign in your given palace and possess your desired place.

Good Morning

Precious one, it is another day of purpose and possibilities!

Let your confidence in God make you feel satisfied with who and what you are!

Although not everything you face today can be changed, nothing can be changed until it is faced!

So go forward, face it, and no matter how challenging it gets …

Never, never, never, give up. It cannot defeat you!

Can you see the win?

I see you at the top where you belong!

Day 14

Even in failure, keep your focus and watch how mockery and ridicule become badges of honor.

I Can't Stop Just Yet

My life has been full of ups and downs,
The journey has been rough and tough.
Enemies have pursued me, and people have betrayed me,
But I have come a long way,
And can't stop just yet.

I have excelled at some endeavors and failed at others,
I've won some battles and I've lost some,
I have embarrassed myself,
I have been mocked and laughed at,
Still, I must forge ahead,
Because I can't stop just yet.

There is so much good in front of me,
I will soon reach the zenith,
I will take the seat on the front row
Where, with a bold and courageous voice,
I will sing my song of VICTORY.

I am winning all the wars.
I am not looking back.
With Jesus before,
I am not afraid.
With the banner before me,
I am sure of victory.
The battle is already won.

Day 15

To be outstanding and fulfill your God given destiny, you must live by two principles. First, do not move or associate with the chickens because they will swallow all your virtues and leave you STRANDED. Second, move with the eagles as they will strengthen your values and watch you SOAR.

Vision

Do you have a vision? Then work it out.

Learn.

Unlearn.

Relearn.

Stretch.

Be curious.

Be challenged.

Take bold steps.

Move with visionaries.

Become purposeful.

Be more.

Reach for the Stars

DAY 16

When you follow defined orders systematically, you will become a mysterious wonder automatically.

Affirmation for Today

I rise; I shine.

I seek; I find.

I work, I increase.

I love God, I follow Him.

I love me; I Love you.

It's my great day.

It's my time.

I receive the best.

I give you the best!

DAY 17

Created in God's image. Equipped with God's reflection.
Designed into God's purpose. Destined for God's glory.

Say It Loud!

I am not an accident,

I am not a disaster,

I am not a failure,

I am a LIFE SEED.

Created intentionally,

Equipped intelligently,

Designed wonderfully,

Destined purposefully.

I am a complex human being.

I am a real essence;

I am one of a kind.

Day 18

No matter how broken or limited you are, you can enjoy life because beautiful things come out of broken pieces.

Hey!

In case you are fallen by the wayside of life,

Dreams and vision shattered, and you are broken inside,

Please do not linger in that place of despair.

Invite the extraordinary One, the God of the universe.

Ask Him to step into the situation and change the status quo.

He will repackage and make you whole again,

For you are His lively seed—a fruitful field.

DAY 19

Remember, you're on a mission; you will manifest your purpose very soon.

Emerge

In this unpredictable moment in time,
I speak to you today, my friend.
You are created, equipped, designed, and destined
To attain whatever you want to have
And become whatever you wish to be.

So let the giant in you rise,
Let the lion in you roar,
Let the champion in you walk,
Let the greatness in you emerge
Till you become a wonder to yourself and to the universe.

Remain at the top!

Day 20

You are God's person, you are God's pilgrim, you are God's platform.
Become like the place you want to go and the person you want to be.

God's Own

Remember you're God's.

You're SPECIAL.

You're a world changer.

Raise your head!

Square your shoulders!

Walk tall!

I see you at your "there."

DAY 21

You're a distinguishing factor. You're a meaningful specific. You're the joy of nations.

Know Yourself

Do you know that you are a COMPLETE SEED?
Created by God,
Equipped by God,
Designed by God,
Destined by God.

Discover yourself,
Discover your gifting,
Discover your skills,
Dominate the world.

You are a SEED.
You are made uniquely,
One in a million.
You are an original.

35

Day 22

*Even when you are broken, God can use you to make others whole
because Jesus does not measure you by your past or potential.
Jesus measures you by the BEST He puts in you and you alone.*

You Are a Seed

Know and believe you are the seed of God.

You are created, equipped, designed, and destined.

Rekindle the passion of your goodness.

Dance to the music of your name.

Become a trademark of significance.

DAY 23

Your life experiences are not meant to impact just your life but others too.

Be Your Authentic Self

Some people in life choose to copy others,
While some choose to live in the shadow of another,
But to live a purposeful and powerful life,
Be your authentic self.

Every one of us has our own uniqueness.
Do not try to be like someone else,
Ignite the flame of your natural essence.
Be your authentic self.

Not everyone will admire or appreciate what you do,
But resolve you will not allow that to distort your focus.
Look forward with vision, insight, hindsight, foresight—
Be your authentic self.

No matter the many trials and obstacles you face,
Regardless of how mean the world you live in may become,
Remaining original is the key to enduring success.
Be your authentic self.

DAY 24

Real life experiences—the power to succeed. I will SEE you at the TOP!

A True Story

Life gave me its blows on every corner
And sent me into the pit of shame and despair,
Still, I chose to rejoice evermore,
Bringing myself to the place of repair.

Although surrounded by darkness then,
My life full of dirt and dust,
I saw no form nor comeliness,
Still, I chose to rise in faith.

I celebrate the victory to start afresh,
For it's my time to rise and shine,
Enlarging the corners of my borders
As I walk and work steadfastly.

Surely, I emerge as a land of gold.
A person of relevance, influence, and affluence,
I majestically take my position at the top,
For that's where I belong.

New Beginning

DAY 25

Character, competence, capability—personal protective equipment for success.

This Is Your Day

You are a price Inestimable,

A Jewel Irreplaceable,

A Life Indispensable,

You are who God says you are.

Today, you may not know where the path will lead,

But you can do what God has given you the capacity to do,

For you know who leads your path.

Today, your eyes are clear

As you take bold steps toward your goals.

Keep shining your destiny-transforming light.

Advance! Achieve! Win! Celebrate!

This is your day.

DAY 26

When you become uncomfortable on your present level, it is time to emerge on your next level.

A New Beginning

It's a new beginning,
It's a fresh start,
It's the planting of a seed,
The watering of life.

See the paths lined with colors,
The air filled with sweet aroma
Revel the radiating beauty it brings.
Enjoy life emerging again.

Today is yours—
Take charge,
Bask in its goodness,
Celebrate it!

DAY 27

Don't be afraid of the stirring of the waters, because it is meant to bring healing. It may be disturbing, it may not be pretty, but it will bring healing.

You Are the Storm

When the battles of life are becoming very fierce,
When the pressures of life are mounting up with force,
When your circle and confidants suddenly turn to foe,
Remember you are the storm.

The storm needs no external support to destroy anything in its path,
The storm needs no pep talk to launch an attack when it is stirred,
The storm takes no command from the organized environment,
The environment trembles at the sound of the storm.

You are the storm.
You are not a victim but a victor;
You are not conquered but a conqueror.
You are not under but on top.

You cannot be assaulted, insulted, or defeated,
You are the STORM.
You are created, equipped, designed, and destined.
You are the STORM!

Day 28

Confidence is feeling blessed for your strengths and weaknesses,
successes and failures, laughter and tears, and messages and messes.

Hold Your Head Up

You are bound to succeed in life.
You will make lots of mistakes,
You will be humiliated one way or another.
You will fail your way to success.

When you go through disappointing moments,
You have nothing to be ashamed of,
There is greatness inside of you,
So hold your head up.

If you ever get discouraged,
If you ever dream and fail,
If everything ever goes wrong,
Still hold your head up.

The troubles of life that do not kill you
Will surely make you stronger.
Get off the mat, look up, and rise!
Hold your head up.

DAY 29

Don't be afraid of doing something new; it may not make sense at first.
If you stay at it much longer, the ray of light will shine on it, you'll get
more clarity. You keep on working at it, and voilà! Success emerges.

Succeed

When life becomes a standstill
And everything becomes a struggle,
You know you can't stay still—
You need to start succeeding.

You may need to change your circle;
You may need to change your companions.
Look for quality people to surround you;
Look for who will help you soar.

Life may not give you what you deserve,
But it will give you what you demand.
Nurture the greatness that's within you,
And nourish the destiny that's already won.

DAY 30

Don't give up in the face of adversity. Destiny is mostly developed in the crucible of trials, temptations, and tribulations.
—Pastor Michael Oladejo, PhD

Life's Walk

You may be walking through the tunnel,

May be standing in the dark,

If you take a moment to focus

And another just to listen,

God may put you to the task.

You receive your deepest message,

You learn your greatest lesson,

You know your truest nature

While walking through the tunnel

And while standing in the dark.

Stop! Look! Listen! Soar!

DAY 31

You are here to discover your own potential and to help others do the same.

Believe Me

My dearest friend,
You are a rainbow after the storm,
You are born to achieve great things in life,
You have the heart of a lion,
You have the spirit of a fighter.

You are amazing and unstoppable,
You are the author of your own success story,
So, no matter the persisting obstacles,
Never, never give up.

God will come through for you;
He will surprise you and support you.
Keep on keeping on, my eagle friend,
The utmost for the best.

DAY 32

Becoming more is not just with words, it requires big dreams, dedication, and big-time determination.

Life

Life is an interesting journey

Full of ups and downs.

Sometimes we win; sometimes we lose.

It's just a learning curve.

When obstacles block your goal,

Keep your head in the game and your heart in the win.

Go forward!

Don't give up!

SUCCEED.

DAY 33

Depression is the killer of destiny. When you are down you cannot dream. Life does not give you what you deserve but what you demand. You must fight to attain your desire.

Don't Waste Your Pain

Life is bright and beautiful,
Yet it comes with good and bad.
Life is rich and wonderful,
But brings its pain along.

Your pain is your peculiarity,
Your pain is your passion,
Your pain is your purpose,
Your pain is your prize.

Your pain is your poise,
Your pain is your possibility,
Your pain is your promise,
Your pain is your progress.

Your pain is your persistence,
Your pain is your prudence,
Your pain is your power,
Your pain is your peace.

Your pain is life's pleasure,
Your pain is your pathway,
Your pain is your praise,
Your pain is your opportunity.

Your pain is God's investment.
It makes you rich and deep,
It brings greatness out of you
And preserves your oil and wine.

Don't waste your pain!

DAY 34

You've been through it to help others live through it. Your story is for His glory.

Your Call; Your Purpose

Everyone has a call;

Everyone has a purpose.

Discover what you are born for,

Discover who you are sent to.

Without finding your call,

Life becomes a loss.

Without fulfilling your purpose,

Life becomes a waste.

You are here to live;

You are made to last.

Wake up to your great, assigned destiny.

Rise up to your God-given ministry.

Manifest! Generations are waiting for YOU!

DAY 35

If you have been refused that does not mean you have been rejected.
You need to relaunch yourself and never weaken your resilience.

Purpose Comes with Pain

Purpose comes with pain;

Your pain is your power.

Pursue your world as it should be,

Don't leave it the way it is.

Life will not always give you what you deserve,

But life will always give you what you demand in prayer.

Put your head in the game.

Never surrender to defeat.

Always, remember,

"This too will pass."

So leave your crown on and keep shining.

I see you at the top!

DAY 36

If you wait for the celebration before you enter the liberation, you are not ready for the elevation.

Do it Well

Your condition doesn't have to be right before you do right.

Your status doesn't have to change before you change your ways.

Your trajectory doesn't have to be perfect before you follow it,

You only need to discover yourself and have the right mindset,

And whatever you do in life, don't just do it, do it well!

DANCE LIKE
NO ONE'S WATCHING
SING LIKE NO ONE'S LISTENING
LOVE LIKE
YOU'LL NEVER BE HURT
PLAY LIKE THERE'S
NO WINNERS
BEHAVE LIKE MOM'S WATCHING
GIVE LIKE YOU HAVE PLENTY
AND SMILE

DAY 37

You may not have anything, but you can still change everything through the power of Jesus Christ that dwells in you.

Your Day

Make your day good,

Make your day count,

Make your day colorful,

Make your day tasteful.

Turn it over to Jesus.

He will remove all obstacles,

He will calm every storm,

He will make all things beautiful.

DAY 38

Not everyone will like what you do but resolve that you will not allow that to determine how you grow. Grow with vision, insight, hindsight, and foresight.

Keep Your Joy

When the details of life appear out of control, keep your joy.

When the results you're expecting are out of your reach, keep your joy.

Joy is not dependent on happenings—it comes from within.

Joy keeps you going with the groaning.

Joy is not man-made, it is divine—from Almighty God.

Keep your joy; live an abundant life.

You are created to be joyful.

DAY 39

Anyone who does not love himself or herself cannot love you. You only get love out of love.

Sow the Seed of Love

Sow the SEED of love.

Make the world a better place.

There is reward in sacrifice,

There is gain in pain,

There is treasure in the trash,

There is hidden fullness in visible emptiness.

So, keep on sowing the seed of love,

Even when unappreciated.

Day 40

In pain, there is purpose. In Christ, there is life. Don't quit, winners don't.

It's Coming to You

There are different seasons in life.
God has made everything beautiful for its own time.
Although he planted the future in your heart,
You cannot see the whole picture of God's work.

You've got to know that no matter what you are up against,
Whatever is happening now, has happened before.
Just trust the process and enjoy the journey,
Believing in the assurance that God is in it!

In crisis, there's courage.
In grief, there's grace.
In fire, there's fragrance.
In misery, there's a message.

In limitation, there is invitation.
In difficulty, there is possibility.
In destruction, there is restoration.
In the ridiculous, there is the miraculous.

My friend, you've got to understand
And keep moving no matter what.

In bitterness, there is sweetness.
In life mundane, there is God ordained.
In ordinary, there is extraordinary.
In fruitlessness, declare your fruitfulness.

In backwardness, there is forwardness.
In barrenness, there is bountifulness.
In the present sighing of pain comes a sudden birthing of joy,
Everything good happening to you at once.

Everywhere there will be blessing!
Unexpected, unexplainable, unpredictable, unprecedented!
Oh my God, blessings! Like wine pouring off the mountains and hills,
So many good things coming fast to you, one after the other.

Stay calm, it's coming to you!

Day 41

*Great Battles? Greater Blessings! Don't give up,
don't give in. Your miracle is on the way.*

Transformed by Grace

I went from crisis to crisis, and in that process,

I discovered myself and found my true friends.

Although tough, I was not just ready to give up.

No, not at all.

I was determined to fight till the battle was won.

This in turn gave birth to all the promotions I had always wanted.

God brought blessings out of brokenness,

Treasure out of trash,

Messages out of messes,

And miracles out of mockery.

Celebration came out of calamity;

Prosperity out of poverty.

Triumph out of tragedy,

Unlimited out of limitations,

And gold out of dust.

God took away all my confusion and gave me clarity,
He moved me from the back seat to a global celebrated spotlight.
God, indeed, changed my stinking story to such a shining glory.

DAY 42

Two things are required to be successful in life: drive and perseverance. You need both.

A Fragrant Woman

A fragrant woman is not a twenty-first century illiterate.
She is always yearning for knowledge.
A fragrant woman loves to learn, unlearn, and relearn.
She favors change over stability.

A fragrant woman wants to arrive at a good place.
She prefers the BEST in everything she does.
A fragrant woman has an eagle's eye,
She sees the world with a 360-degree vision.

A fragrant woman is unashamed of her journey.
She knows her power comes from her pain,
Her strength lies within her scars,
And her passion is her purpose.

Woman! How fragrant are you?

DAY 43

People will see you and treat you the way you see and treat yourself. Always believe that you are peculiar, phenomenal, precious, and priceless no matter what.

A Mother's Announcement

I am a woman, a man with a womb.
I am a mother, a student at the feet of Jesus.
Although I am still learning,
I deliver quality projects on continuous basis.

I carry nations in my womb.
I push them out to existence.
I nurture greatness on my breast
And rock destinies with my hands.

With words, I build palaces and establish authority.
With words, I enthrone kings.
With words, I beautify queens.
And with words, princes and princesses ride on their horses.

With words, I make devil and demons tremble.
With words, I break chains.
With words, strongholds are shattered,
And with words, I bring light to the world.

I am a mother, a student at the feet of Jesus,
Chosen and ordained by God,
Empowered to decree and declare.
Surely with God the Father, Son, and Holy Spirit,
I will succeed in these projects
That will be engraved on the world's "Halls of Fame."

DAY 44

Human opinion is not your identity, you are created, equipped, designed, and destined to burst forth to unimaginable heights and unprecedented glory.

Imperfect Mother

I am a mother.
I am very imperfect but prayerful.
I am very imperfect but purposeful.
I am very imperfect but passionate.
I am very imperfect but praiseworthy.

I am a mother.
I am the undimmed light that brightens the day and the night,
The essential oil that fills the atmosphere with sweet fragrance.
I am the irresistible aroma that everyone long to smell,
The calming voice that diffuses tension and reassures the soul.

I am the comforting hands that support the tired and embrace the weary.
I am an imperfect mother,
Yet I am a do-without.
I am an imperfect mother,
Accepted by the Beloved, celebrated in the world.

DAY 45

*Your life's vision must be backed up with hard work, dedication,
the support of others, and prayer to make it a reality.*

A Daily Prescription

I wake up every single day with a pulse.

And because I have a pulse, I have a purpose.

Today, I fire my passion alive, I pursue my dreams,

I upgrade my self-image, my desire, my calling.

I relocate from the town of hopelessness.

I move to the city of confidence,

Where my faith is made alive,

And I play bigger to better the world.

I am alive. I work out my visions and live out my purpose.

WISE WORDS

Day 46

The infinite mercy of God turns mistakes into miracles, messes into messages, and will turn you into a masterpiece to make you His mouthpiece.

A Parent's Advice

My child,
As you make your way through this world,
With all the dangers and pitfalls it brings,
Have abiding faith in Christ alone.
Believe in His love and care for His own.

When distress, failure, and pain assail,
Call the Shepherd to lead your way.
In times of confusion, doubt, and fear,
Ask the Spirit to clarify.

For in making Him your only source,
You will rise from darkness to light,
A beacon of hope and courage
To a generation so discouraged.

Day 47

Once a SEED is planted, it submits itself to be nourished in the soil.
It does not struggle with itself, its planter, or the environment.
Your word is a SEED, so learn to choose it carefully.

A Mother's Word

As a girl who grew up with the positive and energetic words of her mother,
I know what kind words can do in the life of a child. It never mattered to
my mom what I did or didn't do, she spoke life into me always.
The love my mother lavished on me and my siblings was not earned, it was given to us
free of charge from a graceful heart, a patient heart, and a compassionate heart.
My mother believed I could be anything I wanted to be in life regardless of circumstances. Wow!
The words of my mom were so powerful they are still loud in my ears. The
faith she had in me so great, it's difficult for me to give up in life.
The legacy of my mother is so remarkable, I strive to keep it alive!
And the years I spent with my mom were so beautiful that no tsunami can erase them.
Fellow mothers, give your child prayer, love, attention, and affirmations. Believe
in your child and see through your child with a faith-filled eagle's eye.
Can you see it?
Yes, you're right. I see it too.
A CHAMPION, not perfect but praiseworthy.
Destiny unfolding. Greatness personified!

Day 48

Your association influences your aspirations. Move with the wise, become wiser. Move with achievers, fulfill your potential. Move with visionary minds, set your destiny in motion. Move with small-minded people, die a fool.

Speak and Declare

I'm redeemed by the blood of Jesus.
I'm not cheap, I'm valuable.
I'm a beautiful soul; I have a courageous spirit.
I'm an eagle not a chicken.
I'm a giant in the city; I'm a champion in the land.
I'm not alone; I'm not an accident.
I'm not a failure; I'm not a disaster.
I have a peculiar name.
I have an admirable lifestyle.
I cannot be crushed.
I do not look at myself by reason of size,
I look at myself by reason of my potential.
With Jesus inside me,
No one can intimidate me,
No power can oppress me.
No challenge can silence me.
No darkness can cover me.
I am a masterpiece!

DAY 49

You are designed to discover yourself, uncover your gifts,
use your skills, and dominate the universe.

A Service Creed

My service is not about the people but the purpose.

It's not about the building but the builder.

My service is not about the location but the locator.

It's not about the status but the Savior.

My Service is not about the reward but the Rewarder.

It's not about the glory but the Giver.

So, Lord, in whatever form I render this service,

May I do it in spirit and in truth,

For then I will also receive that which I do not even request.

DAY 50

Your vision is worked out in the place of prayer. You prevail in the place of prayer. The place of strength is the place of prayer.

Mothers in the Land

Lord help us.

Make us the healing hands.

Make us the soothing voice.

Make us the calming embrace.

The smile in a sorry world.

Lord help us.

Let there be peace where we abound.

Let there be hope where we arise.

Let there be joy where we appear,

The strength in a weary soul.

Lord help us.

Make us the warriors of our time,

Standing with humility and grace,

Living out all that God says we are,

The real mothers in the land.

DAY 51

Do you know God loves us all just the way we are?
Don't let anyone tell you otherwise.

My Girl…

You are created an extraordinary champion,
You are a symbol of renewal and rebirth,
You are an embodiment of power, passion, purpose.
You are the fragrance generations love to perceive.

My beautiful girl,
You bring hope to everyone you meet,
Your presence gives strength that livens bones,
Your words keep up the human spirit,
You are a do-without in the world.

My gorgeous girl,
May your rain continue to fall,
May your sun continue to shine,
May your rainbow continue to color the earth,
May the graceful Lord continue to carry you.

Day 52

Do not focus on the current formlessness in your journey, just celebrate the meaning you have brought to the world. As you keep navigating the roadblocks, you will make your way to the finish line.

A Letter from the Heart

My precious son and daughter,

As you wait on the Lord for your hearts' desires,

Let the GRACE of Jesus Christ be sufficient for you.

No matter the shape and size of life's challenges,

Don't compromise your faith. HOLD ON!

Don't allow miserable comforters derail you from reliance on God. Choose godly circle!

Don't seek other alternatives in life, Jesus is the real deal!

Don't yield to worldly and ungodly counsel, instead, ask the HOLY SPIRIT!

Don't disrespect and devalue your spouse. Be very wise not a fool!

Don't spoil your children, but love and train them!

Don't be arrogant or proud; God only promotes humble people!

Above all, be BORN AGAIN. It's your only way to heaven!

DAY 53

Don't be prideful but be confident in who you are. Don't be perfect but be praiseworthy. Be satisfied with your self-worth and be pleased by the work of your hands.

Seven of Life's Do-Nots

- Do not allow past embarrassing experiences define and limit your natural, real essence. Learn from your past and move forward.
- Do not allow your fears get the best of you. Face your fears.
- Do not be missing in action. Always know that there is destiny at stake for any action or inaction.
- Do not allow the many stops and detours before your destination discourage you. Keep your focus.
- Do not be threatened by the mistakes and fake lifestyles you see around you. Be strengthened as you go from being a mess to becoming a masterpiece.
- Do not be perfect. Be praiseworthy, disciplined, determined, and dedicated. Do your best. Do it well!
- Do not live a lie. Be free. Be real. Be you!

DAY 54

*Follow God. Follow your dreams, and do not conform to
the norm. Dare to be different. Dare to be YOU!*

To My Sister, the Queen

My Sister—Queen, warrior, voice,

You've got inner beauty,

You've got inner strength,

Make sure you know who you are.

Always be your genuine self.

Don't be defined by what you see around you,

Be defined by what God says about you.

You know what?

God says you are created to be more, more than you can be.

Smile! Stride! Shine! Soar!

I see you at the top.

Day 55

When you don't get a miracle, God can still use you as a miracle for someone else.

Guard It

Guard the grace you carry.

You're a divine messenger to the world.

You're a distinguishing factor.

You're a meaningful specific.

Guard your space.

Day 56

We won't always understand the timing of God, yet we can yield to the timing of God. Living our lives according to the will of God is what we are supposed to do. God's timing will help us to enjoy the journey and not focus on the goal itself.
—Lois Oladejo

You Are God's

You are God's person.

You are God's project.

You are God's pilgrim.

You are God's purpose.

You are God's property.

You are God's platform.

You become like the place you want to go.

You become so closely like the person you want to be.

STRIDE! The zenith is yours.

I celebrate you there!

DAY 57

Life is hard? Yes, I know! But you still need to get at it because only failures give excuses for their failure. The great ones turn it around to their advantage.

Take Me under Your Wings

I've been through so much till now.
Still, I can't give up just yet.
When the going gets very tough,
Lord, take me under Your wings.

The battles of life are raging.
The billows of life assailing;
The burdens of life abounding.
Lord, take me under Your wings.

In the moments when I feel all alone,
Still, I know that God is for me.
I find inner peace and rest in the storm.
As You take me under Your wings.

Under Your wings, my strength is renewed.
Under Your wings, my purpose is fulfilled.
Under Your wings, my destiny is evolving.
Lord, keep me under Your wings.

Day 58

Brokenness doesn't mean the sun won't shine again. Today, you are a land of dust, but very soon, you will be a land of gold.

Hear This

Although you are created, equipped, designed, and destined,

You are called to SERVE humanity with everything in you.

And though your place of service now may be OBSCURE,

Keep SERVING diligently and dedicatedly,

It will soon lead you to STAND on the pedestal of RELEVANCE and INFLUENCE.

Because in GREATNESS, you serve your way to the top.

DAY 59

Living under the pretence that all is well doesn't allow a person the pleasure of getting the help he needs.

A Deep Desire for God

Lord, my spirit is dissatisfied because I have a longing for more.

I want God and His presence to make me what I ought to be.

I want the "new" to happen to me, my life to start again.

I want old patterns removed, old foundations destroyed,

My eyes to open to the light of God's glory.

Lord, my spirit is dissatisfied because I have a longing for more.

I want my water to turn to wine, a transition to happen in my spirit.

I want the presence of God, a desire for a superior spiritual dimension.

I want the desires of the spirit, a strengthening of the inner man,

My ears to open to the voice of God's guidance.

Lord, my spirit is dissatisfied because I have a longing for You!

DAY 60

Do you know God loves us all just the way we are?
Don't let anyone tell you otherwise.

God Bless You

May your rain continue to fall.

May your sun continue to shine.

May your rainbow continue to color the earth.

May the Lord carry you!

May the Lord bless you and keep you.

May the Lord turn His favor toward you.

May the Lord be gracious to you.

May He give you peace!

Bonus

In the next few lines, as a bonus, I'm sharing the ABC'S of your identity to help enhance your thought, build your faith, and gain confidence in life. The list of positive adjectives will encourage you to use your words to reinforce your world.

Stay blessed and remain positive.

THE ABC'S OF YOUR IDENTITY

A: acceptable, accomplished, admirable, adopted, adorable, affluential, alive, alluring, ambassador, amiable, amazing, amazon, angelic, anointed, appealing, appointed, articulate, attractive, authentic, awesome

B: beacon, beaming, beautiful, beloved, best among equals, best in who I am, best where I am, bestie, big, bigger, biggest, blameless, blooming, blossoming, blessed, bold, bouncy, bountiful, brave, brightening, brilliant

C: calm, capable, captivating, career orientated, caring, celebrated, champion, charming, chosen, classy, comely, commander, compassionate, complex, collage of beauty, confident, conscientious, courageous, creative, cute

D: daring, daughter of Zion, dazzling, delightful, dependable, designed for power, desirable, destined to win, detail oriented, determined, dignified, disciplined, distinct, distinctly different, distinguished, distinguishing factor, dynamic

E: eagle, eclectic, elected, elegant, elite, embodiment of wisdom, empathetic, empowered, energetic, epitome of grace, esteemed, excellent, exceptional, exemplary, extraordinary, extraordinary ambassador

F: fabulous, fantabulous, fantastic, faithful, fascinating, fashionable, favoured, fearless, ferocious warrior, focused, force to reckon with, forceful, forgiven, fragrant influence, free, friendly, fruitful

G: generational landmark, generous, genius, gigantic, godly, God's poetry, God's story, good enough, good looking, global joy, glorious, gorgeous, graceful, gracious, grandeur, great

H: head, helpful, here to stay, holy, honest, honorable, hospitable, humble

I: icon, iconic, incredible, indescribable, indestructible, indomitable, Industrious, influential, ingenious, illustrious, innovative, inspirational, intelligent, imaginative, impactful, important, impressive, irreplaceable, irresistible

J: jewel, jolly, joy of many generations, joyful, joyous, jubilant, judicious, just, justified

K: king, knight, knowledgeable

L: large, laudable, leader, legend, liberated, life force, light, lively, living soul, lovable, loved, lovely, loving

M: magnificence, majestic, man of valor, marvellous, masterpiece, me, meaningful, meaningfully specific, mighty, model, modern, motivational, multitasker

N: natural, new, nice, noble, normal, nurturing

O: one in a million (not one *of* a million), one of a kind, open to the Word of God, optimistic, organized, original, overcomer

P: paragon of excellence, passionate, patience, peaceful, peculiar, perfection, persistence phenomenal, plenipotentiary ambassador, poise, positive, powerful, praiseful, praiseworthy, prayerful, preferred, prestigious, pretty, priest, principled, promising, prosperous, prudent, purposeful

Q: queen, qualitative-essence, quality, quintessential

R: rare-combination, real, realistic, reconciled, redeemed, relevant, reliable, remarkable, resilient, resourceful, respectful, responsible, revelational, revolutionary, rich, righteous, royal

S: sassy, seek out, self-worth, shining star, significant, significantly relevant, simple, skillful, smart, special, spectacular, strong, stunning, stylish, subject matter, successful, supernatural

T: talented, tasteful, tenacious, thoughtful, tough, trailblazer, transformational, transformed, treasure, trendy, triumphant, truthful

U: unafraid, undaunting, understanding, unicorn, unique, universal appeal, unlimited, unbeatable, undefeated, undeniable, unforgettable, unshakable, unstoppable

V: valiant, valuable, valued, victorious, virtuous, visionary, voice

W: warrior, wealthy, welcoming, winner, wise, wonderful, worthy, worshipper of God

X: xenial

Y: young, youthful

Z: zazzy, zeal, zealous, zestful

Be Encouraged

If you have endured ridicule and/or shame because of your weaknesses or the trials and tempests
you have suffered in life, I have this joyous news for you from 2 Corinthians 12:10: "I am at
peace and even take pleasure in any weaknesses, insults, hardships, persecutions, and afflictions
for the sake of the Anointed because when I am at my weakest, He makes me strong."
My friend, do you know that your weaknesses, trials, pains, tribulations, and so
on provide you with opportunities to showcase God's grace and power?
You see, there are so many people suffering in this world today but are
afraid to share their stories because they fear criticism from others, have
unrealistic emotional expectations, feel inadequate and not enough.
Be very careful not to feel ashamed to talk about your real journey and vulnerabilities. Hear me! When
you talk about your wounds and reveal your scars, you are comforting others who suffer and feel alone.
2 Corinthians 1:3-4 says, "All praise goes to God, Father of our Lord Jesus, the Anointed One. He is
the Father of compassion, the God of all comfort. He consoles us as we endure the pain and hardship
of life so that we may draw from His comfort and share it with others in their own struggles."
You went through it so you could pull others through it. There are people out there who will find value
in your story. Prayerfully look for them to add meaning to their lives today. Share your story and be
original about it. Turn your weakness to strength. Become a healer. Give hope in a hopeless world.
God bless you as you bring joy to others.

Printed in the United States
by Baker & Taylor Publisher Services